DAVID FICKLING AND PERRY HINTON
THE PATH OF PERIL
ILLUSTRATED BY
RACHEL BIRKETT

TREASURE HUNTER WANTED. Resourceful treasure seeker required. Able to travel immediately. Chances of survival slim. Rewards for success beyond your wildest dreams. Faint hearts need not apply. Box No. 4895

PUFFIN BOOKS

You notice a curious advertisement in *The Times* for a treasure hunter and decide to apply. By return of post you receive a letter from a Mr Hardbinder of City of London solicitors Messrs Cobb and Hardbinder, inviting you to their offices the next day. There is no further explanation, but included with the letter is a newspaper cutting.

Mysterious Death of Famous Explorer

Mr Edmund Mallory, the world-famous explorer, was found dead in his study yesterday morning by his housekeeper, Mrs Ethel Baker. Mysterious circumstances surround his death. According to the police, Mrs Baker has been admitted to hospital suffering from shock. The police have sealed off the house but refuse to comment further except to say that foul play is suspected and that they are looking for a person of unnatural physical strength.

Mr Mallory was to have addressed a meeting of the Royal Geographical Society in Kensington Gore tonight describing his recently successful and daring expedition to the Far East. A spokesman for the Society said last night that Mallory was to have announced a discovery of immense importance. His secret may now be buried with him as he had taken no one into his confidence.

At eleven o'clock the next morning you find yourself in a cab seated beside Mr Hardbinder. You are surprised that Hardbinder seemed to accept you for the job without asking any questions or knowing anything about you. In fact he bundled you into this cab with almost indecent haste, but your fears are allayed by Hardbinder's friendly and businesslike manner. During an otherwise silent journey he passes you a letter and says uneasily, 'Edmund Mallory, the explorer, left instructions that in the event of his sudden and violent death an advertisement was to be placed in *The Times*'s Personal Column. This letter will explain what is required of you. Should you decide not to take this commission, I will instruct the cabbie to drive back.'

As the cab makes its way through the mid-morning traffic you read the letter.

Dear Friend,

When you read this letter I shall be dead. Understand also that if you take on this quest, then that which has killed me will as surely try to destroy you. It is a malicious power from whose vengeance there is no safe place in this world or the world to come; and I am asking you to seek it out in the very heart of its evil domain. My hope is that you will not be deterred, but I beg you to be warned and be ever vigilant.

Some months ago I embarked on a secret expedition to the roof of the world. This journey was the culmination of a life's work. I told no one and left with the minimum of fuss, carrying very little equipment and depending on local help where necessary. My goal was one of the great mysteries of the world. I have many times in my travels come across the legend of a lost land in the high mountains, of an ancient civilization and a fabulous treasure – a jewel known as the Bloodstone and said to have strange powers.

By a stroke of good fortune I obtained a fragment from an ancient map which seemed to point to the exact geographical location of the treasure. After making careful plans I left to seek out the lost land and learn its secrets.

In my eagerness I had ignored all the warnings left by the ancients. In particular I had chosen not to notice the references to the 'Guardian of the Jewel' who, according to legend, would hunt down and destroy any who sought to steal the Bloodstone. I could not believe in such mystical nonsense.

It was a long journey to the end of my quest. I encountered many dangers and saw sights the like of which I would ask no man to believe who had not seen them with his own eyes. And in the end I held the jewel in my own hands and took it from its resting place and brought it back to this country.

From the moment I possessed the jewel I had no peace. Both my dreams and waking hours were haunted by a monstrous creature. I slept little and many times thought I had seen the Guardian watching me at the edge of my vision. I know the creature has followed me back to this country and I know it just waits for the time to wreak its vengeance and take back the jewel.

Since then I have buried myself in researches to discover if there is a way to free myself from the curse. To no avail. I am doomed. Too late I learned that I could have avoided the curse if only I had possessed the Mask of the Guardian and known the demon's true name. But that knowledge will not save me now.

I have written the secret of the jewel and its Guardian in a notebook. The notebook contains a hidden message – all the information needed to retrieve the jewel and lift the curse. To safeguard my secret from the greedy and ignorant, the notebook will give up the knowledge only to the most resourceful adventurer.

This is the task I ask of you. The way has many perils but the rewards are beyond compare. If you will take on this task, my life's work will not have been in vain and an ancient evil will have been exorcised and my soul redeemed. My solicitor will give you access to my diary, a map and the notebook. Use them to find the treasure, I beg you. There is nothing left for me. I await the Guardian. I am afraid for my soul.

Edmund Mallory

As you read the letter, your curiosity and sense of adventure are aroused. You are determined to undertake this quest, and you ask Hardbinder for the notebook, diary and map. He smiles, saying, 'I am afraid you will have to wait until we reach our destination,' and, shaking you warmly by the hand, 'but I am so glad you have decided to accept.'

Soon you arrive at the explorer's house in Kew and are shown into Mallory's study, the scene of his death. Nothing has been moved and you are shocked at the sight before you. Hardbinder tells you that the torn fragments of paper are all that is left of the diary, but that the notebook and map are fortunately intact. There is no sign of the Bloodstone. Whoever or whatever murdered Mallory seems to have taken the jewel as well. First you examine what is left of the diary. It seems to be a log of Mallory's journey, though the text has a mass of strange symbols scattered through it. Next you study the small notebook. Inscribed on the opening page is a strange message and a curious sign, while the second page contains an enigmatic instruction.

> The Sign of the Guardian.
>
> Here are the twelve perils. Those who would learn how to defeat the Guardian and win the Bloodstone must follow my journey exactly.

> Read the first of the first, the second of the second and continue until the journey is ended. Then take the last of the last and so on until the journey is begun.

The remainder of the notebook is composed of twelve separate entries. Each entry refers to a particular peril or danger faced by Mallory on his quest for the Bloodstone. The entries seem in no particular order. You will have to place the perils in the correct order before you can discover the answer to the riddle of the notebook.

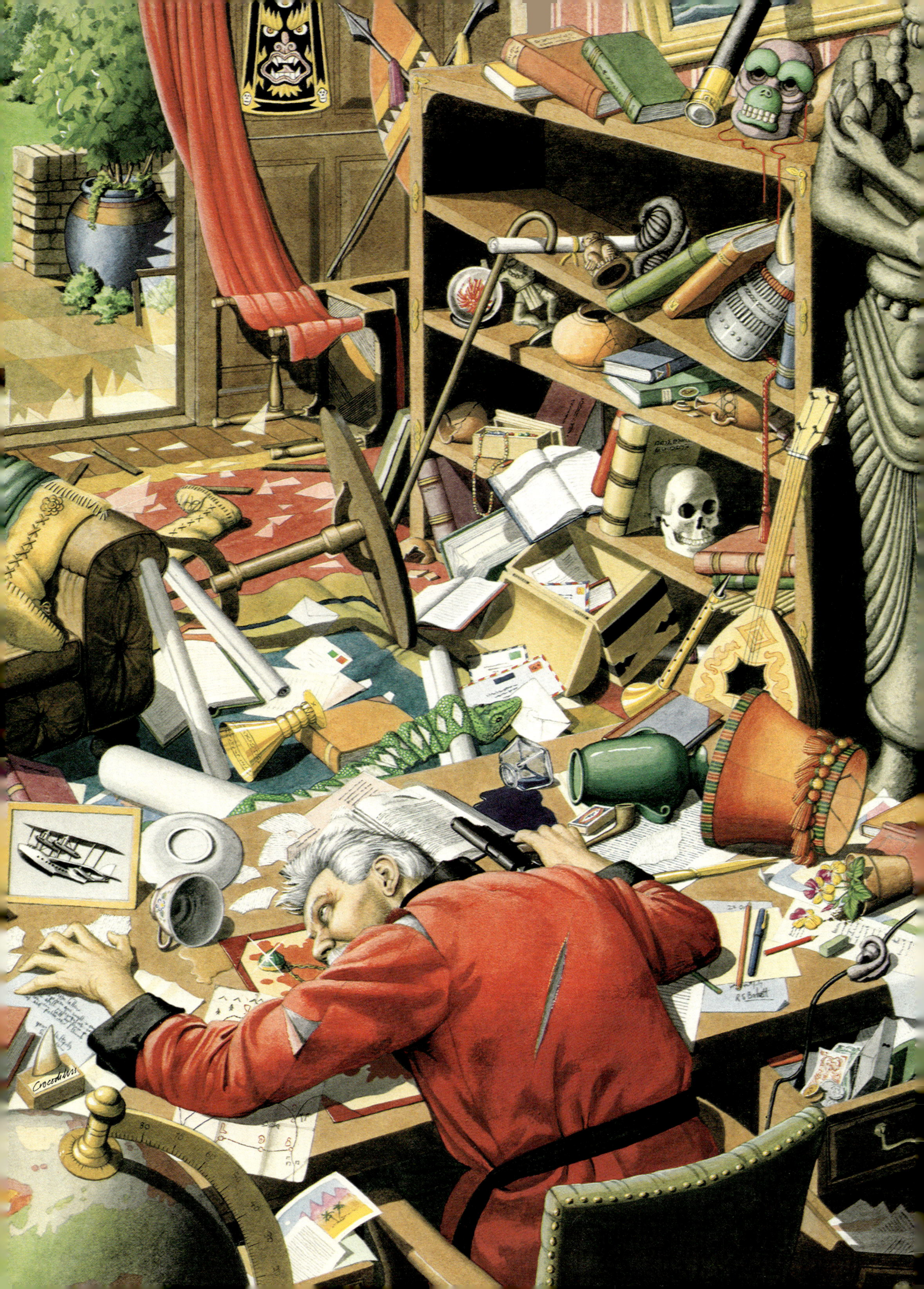
Crocodilus

The map makes more sense. The route of the explorer's journey can be traced easily enough. However, there are no place names. Instead small hieroglyphs mark the route. Clearly, these hieroglyphs show the location of the twelve perils the explorer had to face. You are pondering what the hieroglyphs represent when Hardbinder tells you that Mallory brought back twelve artefacts from his journey and that they are still present in the study. Surely the hieroglyphs must represent these artefacts?

Your first task is clear. You must match each of the map hieroglyphs to an artefact in the study. Afterwards, you realize, you will have to travel to the East, following in the explorer's footsteps to discover where each of the artefacts came from. With this knowledge you will be able to place the twelve perils in the order shown by the map. Only then will you be able to decipher the notebook and learn its secret.

After you have fully investigated the study and its contents you prepare for your journey. Hardbinder takes care of your expenses and travel arrangements, and soon you find yourself in the comfort of an Imperial Airways flying boat travelling to the East. From now on you are on your own.

Do you have the necessary courage and resourcefulness to follow the path of peril? Will you survive the twelve perils and reach your goal alive? And if you do, will you discover the whereabouts of the Bloodstone? Or will you become another victim of the jewel's terrible Guardian?

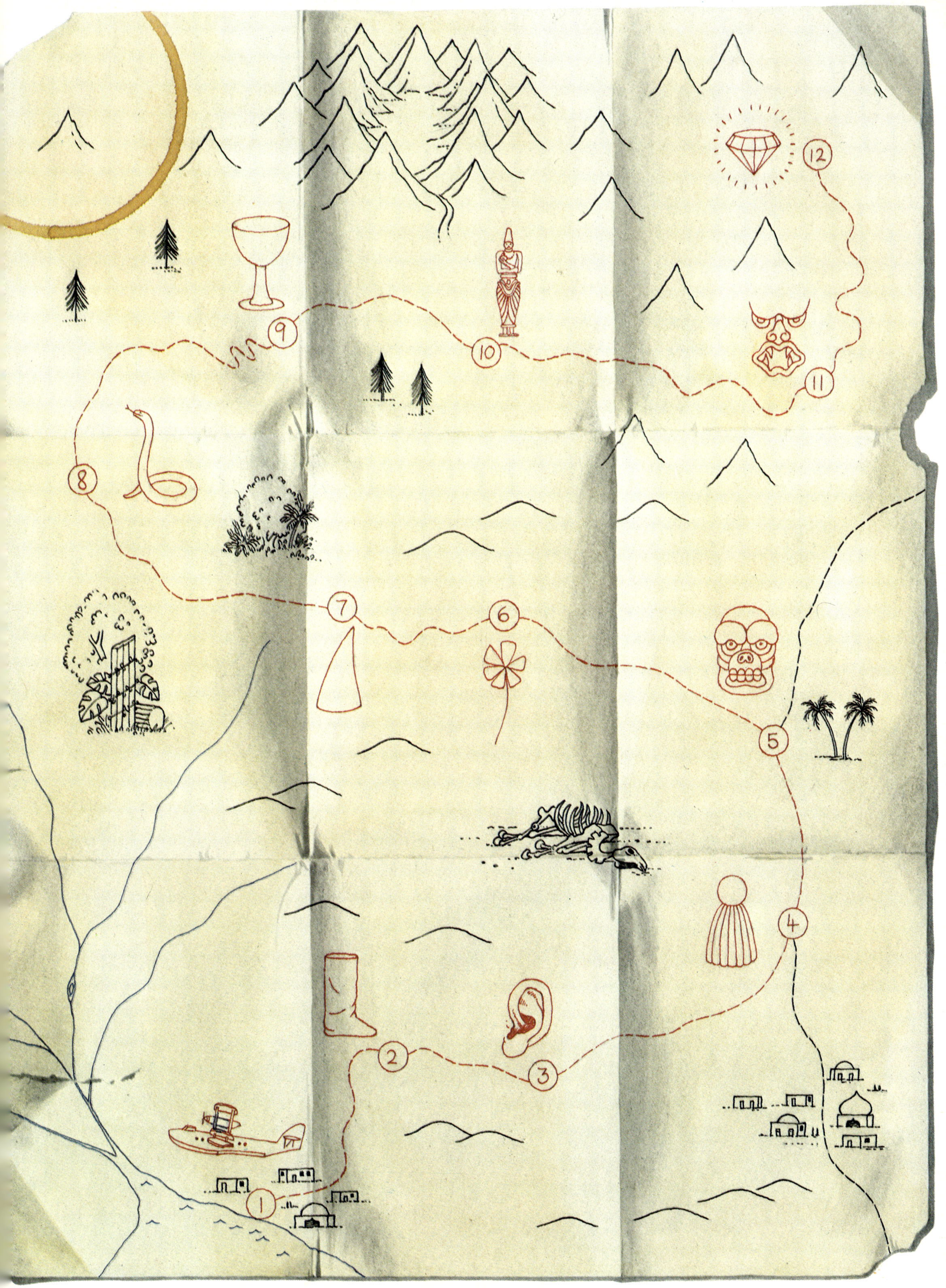

1
2
3
4
5
6
7
8
9
10
11
12

...dge. Her words...
...Master of the Bridge. No on...
...his behest.' The silent temple a...
...ge seemed empty and the bridge lay
...ly near, but we hesitated to cross. An
...air broken only by the
...gentle breeze. 'Look!'
...emerged a strange
...ng a small dr...

...tantalizing...
eerie stillness filled t...
creaking of the bridge in the
cried Ryecart. From the temple
figure, one of their priests, tapp...
'Banhar, Banhar, Protector of
His hypnotic chanting he...
Suddenly a raucous...
cackling broke th...
...ning red-eyed ap...
...ssued from
...' we

...all, Banhar, D...
...d us transfixed.
...-pitched screeching
...ell. A horde of
...tures, their fangs
...s 'Run!'...

...main behind the...
...yself up towards the opening...
...s there — the Hall of Incandescence...
vantage point I could see the lights...
throbbing with a mystic power, drawing...
to the ancient altar which I recognised...
Incarcerated Quarghur — immortal...
Old Ones. Red-eyed ape creatures...
...thing in silent horror... As...

...e my uncontrolled min...
the awakening Quarghur, life...
subconscious they strove agains...
unequal but before I lost con...
figure of a man rising from...
I awoke among my...
safety...

...g my eyes...
...zed as the...
...l enemy of the...
...clung to its sides,...
...I stared upon...
...d was assailed by...
...serpents of the...
...t me. The struggle was...
...sciousness I saw the...
...the altar. To my relief...
...Fearing fo...

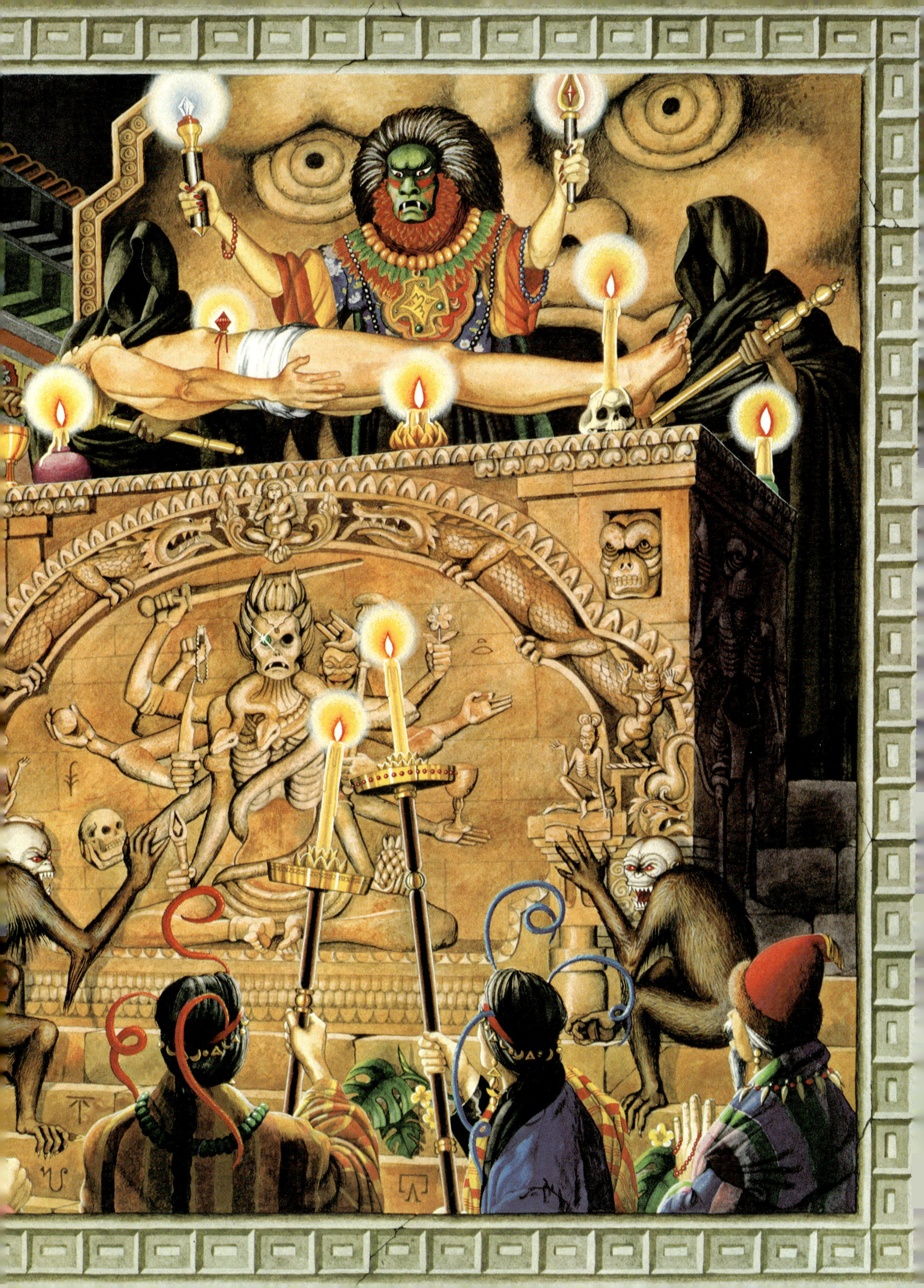

only sman's
this morning a huge cl...
above us. Luckily one of the gua...
up and cried out. We had bare...
leap out of the way before the
us. No one was hurt — but ...
ponies stumbled and fe...
afternoon we had r...
the Thousand ...
As we crossed
to us and

...n its panic...
...into the abyss. By...
...ached the upper ledge...
...teps. The tower rose high at...
...the ice ledge the guide ahead...
pointed at something hi...
...inside. But before we...
...ing cry pierced the...
...horror the sn...
...d he dis...

...one of the...
...rashed beside...
...ly enough time to...
...des had been looking...
...ty of ice gave way...
...ock and snow but...
...have been the avalan...
...ow thick sheets...
...e most ar...

caught
nofurther. He
nge fire, selecting only
He then drew runes on th
d us not to stray from the
e wild creatures in these
ars, but I fear the guide did
. I slept fitfully that night.
red in my ears urging me
denly I awoke to the
companions had
as we dared
Strange sounds. Th
Echoing Hills. He to
hear are the spirits
'Taker but would expla
ssuaded to make a
woods to burn.
rocks and warm
fire until dawn. There a
ts, wolves and b
of them
ices whisper
quest. Sudde
ing me. One of my
We searched as far
not be found.
Cress and the fire w
we huddled round the e

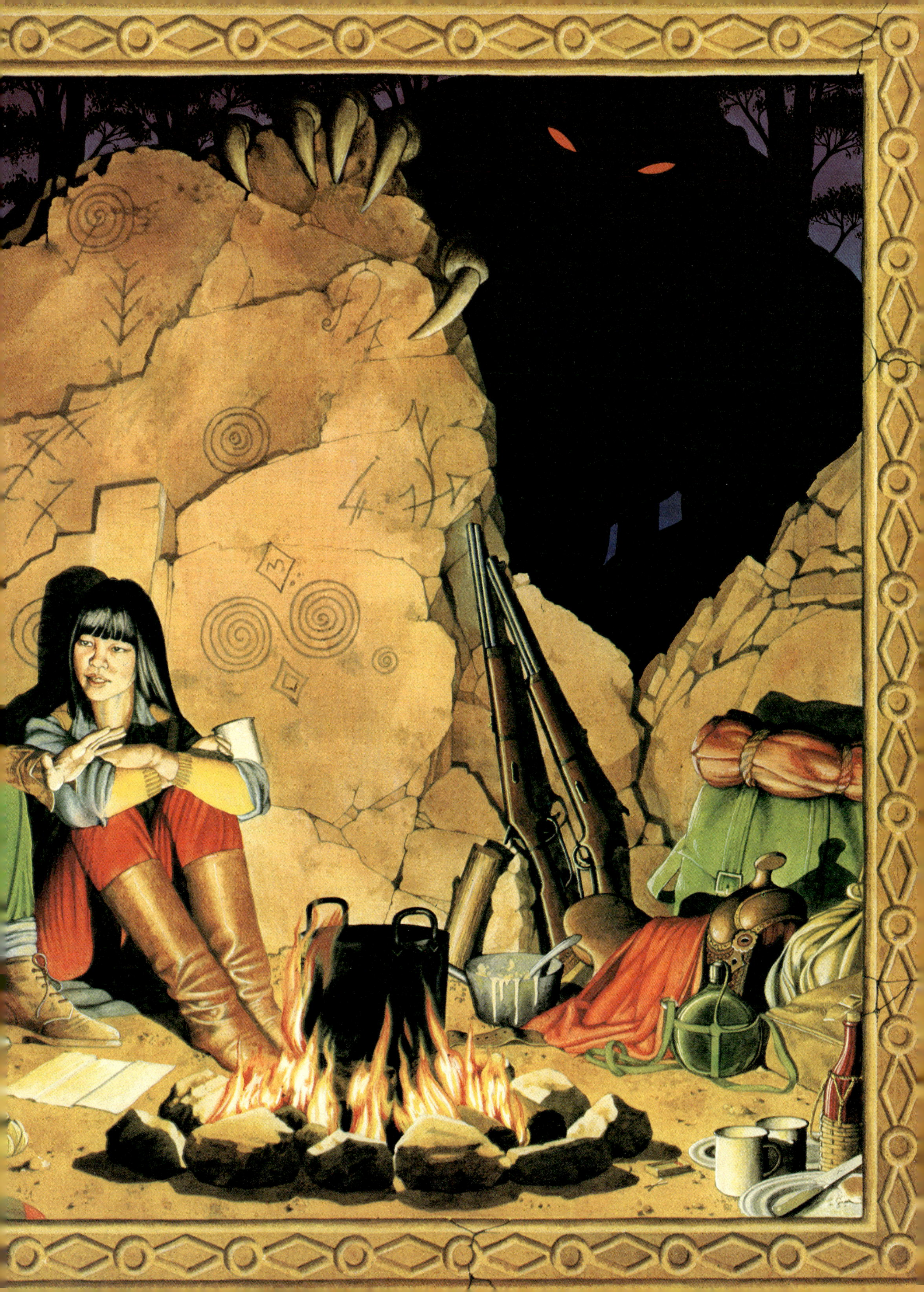

...wizard was raging...
...was held by my companion...
...gates are warded by the Ol...
...the female warrior, snarled.
...can open them and resist u...
...faced th... Many have...
...e in Pa...

...overwhelmed me. ...sh pulled me back. ...od and struggling. The ...out me once more and I ...'Fool. These ...Ones,' Karin-da, ...'No mortal ...less he has first ...died on these steps ...Then she gave ...dfolded.

bulk of the gates...
open effortlessly with just...
steel still. The blizzard was ga...
eternal summer. A great longi...
Old Ones in their golden city...
"...someone cried and I was...

Suddenly we
saw before us —
we saw from the massive
the Old Ones. We were on
the Road of All Souls.
Spot, each chasing the others
An eerie light issued from
of which stood a massive
urge came upon me
started for

the ceremonial path —
tired by the acolytes of the
all of his earthly possessor
om the temple, at the heart
ificent there. An irresist-
ake my place upon it
ully I was t

an ancient tem
sun, but I saw
heads that it was
of the Skull — one of

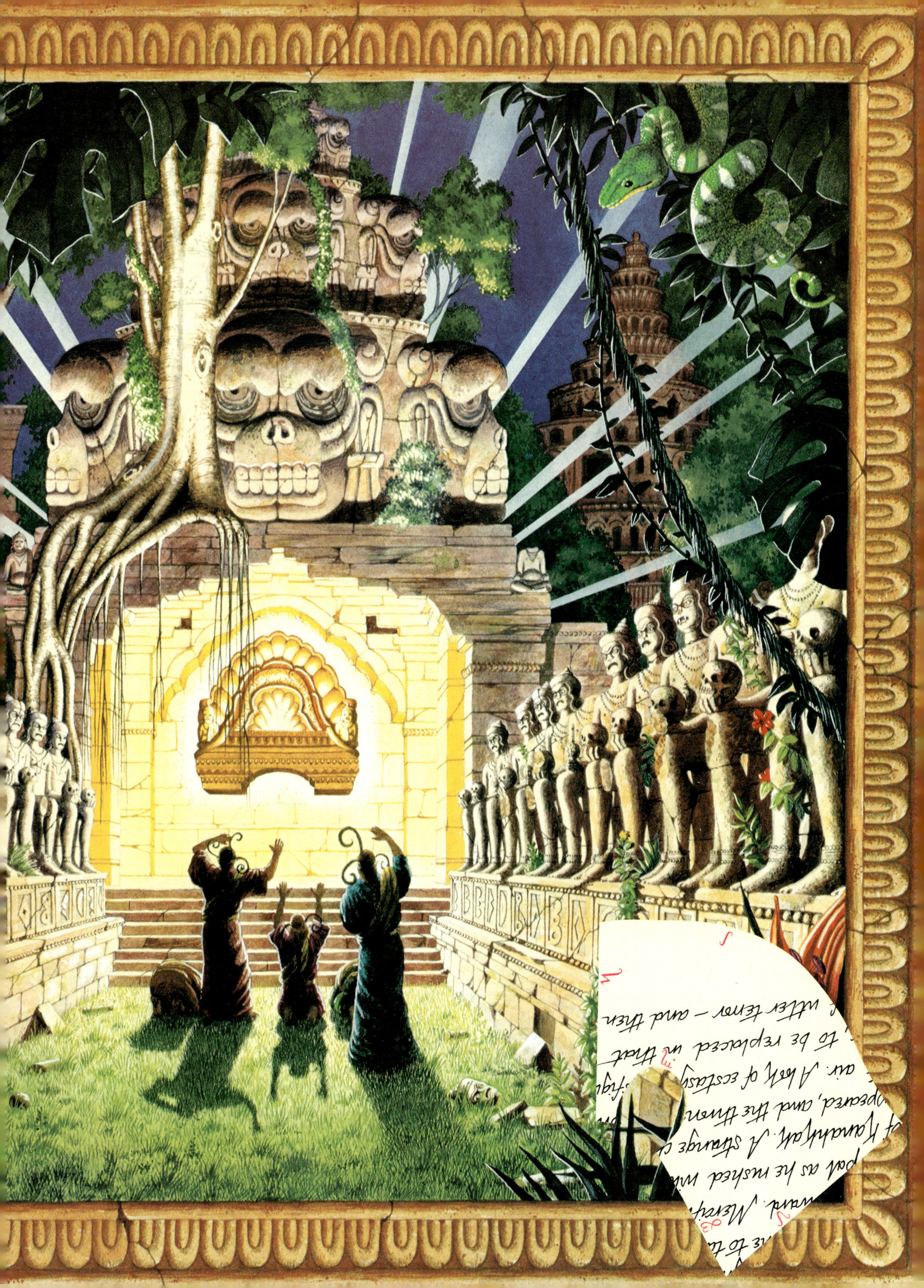

back str...
he paced...
he counselled...
from the high country ha...
city and they are feared
See the man with the cla...
arrival? Trust no one...
We left the agent's of...
our gear and preparin...
As we made our wa...
streets (atuna...)
"Over there."

through th...
tugged at my...
Standing apa...
ue man with a ...ch ha...
ow searching the cr...
...better make haste," I urged.

...ever. Tak...
d powerful people in the o...
ve been seen in the not
...by all. Did you not
...by observing your
...there are spies everywhere
...intent on collecting
...for an early departure
...the throng...

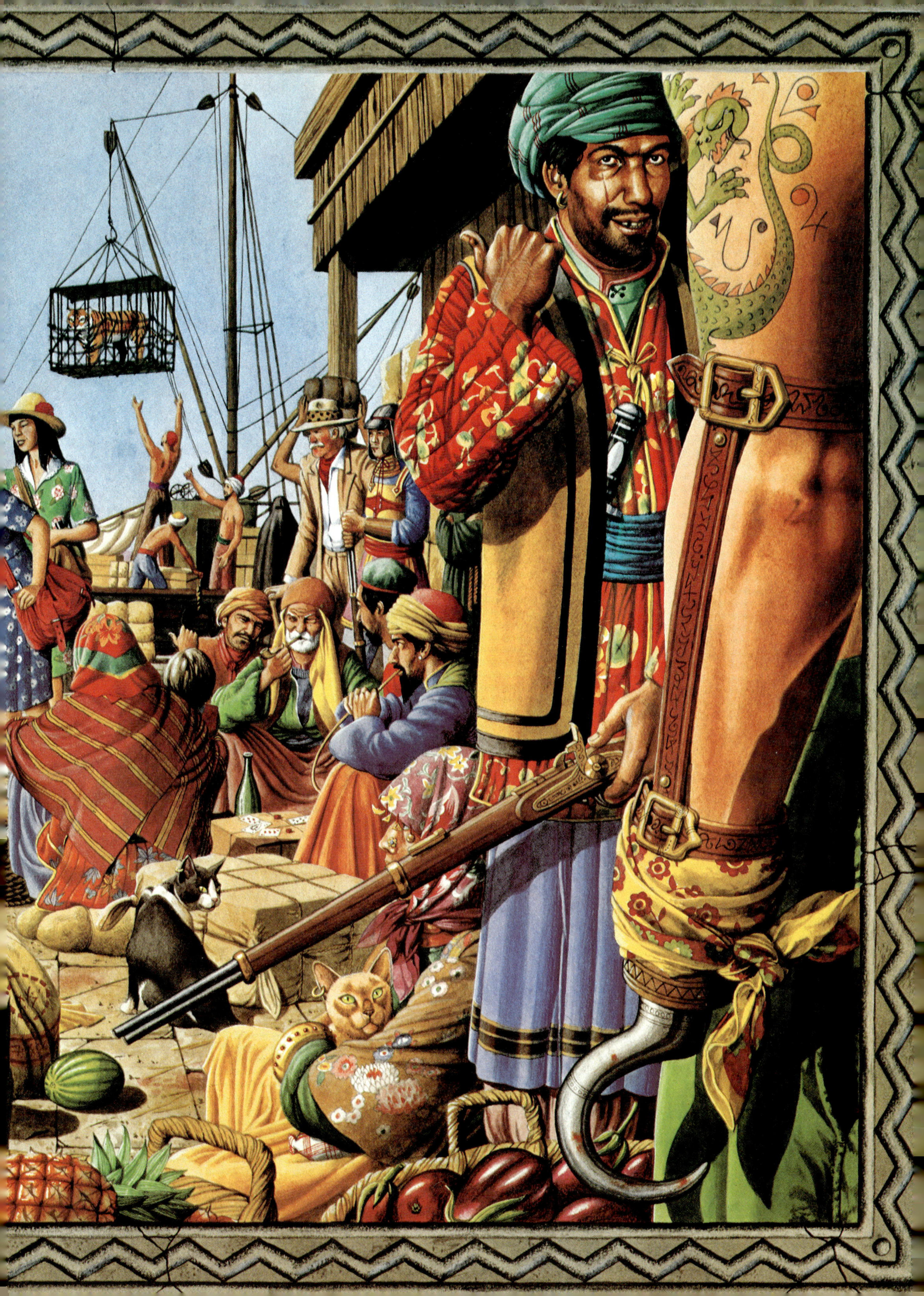

...ud, 'as gifts...
We must give him so...
red Catuna. 'Wait,' cried...
ing we could offer could...
agnificent gifts, oh nob...
ccept your bounty...

us rise and accomp...
Yacood. Before us was a...
aching into the flames to pu...
t brand. 'Had we offered anything,...
ued, 'the reward for our insult w...
suffer that. It is only after...
that a warrior will attempt the...
the warrior priests are chose...
the hand but those...

match y...
ble lord. We humb...
The warlord smiled, ...
many him. 'Look,' sai...
brazier with a war...
uck out...

them. May they s
priest still watches. Be
scampered back into the
was gone. Gingerly we cre
made
the golden coins
ked us and gave us
of my people once lived
ned away from Amanal
from the river. We dare not
for fear of the Old One. Take
serve you well, but Amanal's
the river. Then he
gloom of the caves and
into the light and
bank towards the boats.

...ound began...
...n the darkness. A...
...ooded the cave and w...
...faces. We had reached...
...a huge waterfall thun...
...Mordip turned to...
...and we gave him...
...promised. He tha...
...of warning. "Man...
...here but we tu...
...and he cast us...

harm me..." ...urn before
on the boy and gave him... ...d myself...
which he accepted eager... ...chin. "Do not
was drawn to a stall se... ...implored. I took pity
artefacts, charms, effigies... ...r a small silver coin,
of the Old One Kanadhya... ...ly. My attention
about to begin haggling... ...lling unusual
a boy's voice cried out:... ...and carvings
"A hooded one!" I s... ...as I was
...raised knife a... ...tall`nSider
...isted in a g... ...Maste

Just c...
with the ...
Watch out ...
ran round to c...
a hideous ...
rimace of hate.
lethal blade a...
a hooded cloak ...

"From his   e air
of the Desert Bull!"
              ... as a mass of wild
         om the dunes towards us.
       ed from the sun. 'Come,
          tugging at my
            e after human spoi...
           made to unbuckle m...
              firmly and hiss...
                 reluctantly I...

When
       scanning the
        were nervous. We
          he explained, encamp...
           Torran, the Desert Bull, wh...
             souls of his enemies.' A scre...
              and one of the outriders toppl...
               camel. 'Miss! The riders
               cried the caravan mas...
                horsemen swept down f...
                 their scimitars glinting
                  Master!', shouted
                    mel's halte...

and why they
Jacord the Black Oasis,
the servants of
feasts on the
am pierced th

shadows loomed in the
and I ran. There was no
place for the bindings lay in
for I wondered what
to such a fate.
my unspoken question
custom of the people
this land belongs

The Visitation.
The diary holds the secret of the Taker who stalks these hills. There are safe places to camp known only to the guides. The Taker will not prey upon those who stay close to the sacred fire after dusk.

The Thunderer.
Beneath the mighty waterfall follow the sign of the crocodile, it will lead you to the river dwellings and the boats you must use. They are dedicated to the crocodile god Amanal and are adorned with his most sacred symbols. He has cursed these waters.

The Assassin.
Then you must journey to the bazaar at Molglos where the eyes of many enemies will be upon you. Be on your guard especially for the knives of the hooded Merchants of Hos who make their living by dealing in your death.

The Claw-Handed Man.
Trace your path with care traveller and beware the man with the claw. He watches the harbour for those who do not worship at the altar of the Old Ones and rob this land of its treasures.

The Human Sacrifice.
The ancient fragment of map shows a ruined city where the Old Ones still come to accept the sacrifice of their worshippers. This is an evil place. Do not remain here during the hours of darkness.

The Cry of the Guardian.
Any sound in these mountains causes huge avalanches to fall, making the route treacherous. A bloodcurdling cry is often heard above the Thousand Steps where the ice ledge and the ramparts of the high tower join. Beware!

The Altar of the Quarghur.
Strange visions assail your mind forming and coalescing like a spectral jigsaw. Only the priest may command these visions into the image of the Old One. Should an untrained mind attempt the feat the Quarghur's evil apparition will materialise from the pieces.

The Gates of the Forbidden Land.
You need guidance to pass through the gates without peril. Manat's power is here, it will take your mind and leave your body to rot. Only those who have been trained by fire can lead the way; follow in their footsteps or perish by the wayside.

The Fire Ceremony.
Though fierce and warlike the warrior people treat each traveller to their lands in the same manner. They will offer you gifts which must be accepted. Beware! Give them nothing, even if they demand gifts of matching value in return.

The Servants of Banhar.
By the chasm lies the guardian's temple. Though silent and apparently deserted this temple is occupied by the Watcher of the Bridge. She calls to the Servants of Banhar to destroy all travellers attempting to cross.

The Throne of Kanahkak.
The ruined palace of Kanahkak will lie on your route. Do not approach by the Road of All Ends else a terrible compulsion to sit upon the throne may overwhelm you. Of those that succumb no fragment will be left behind.

The Caravan of Many Deaths.
The desert tribe closest to the route of the caravans are the followers of the Old One Torran. They will approach from the south and mask their murderous attack with the glaring midday sun.